BROMYARD

THE DAY BEFORE YESTERDAY

A book of photographs

Published by Bromyard & District Local History Society
1979

 ©

ISBN 0-9502068-1-4

Printed by Print Logic, Foley Estate, Hereford.

INTRODUCTION.

As long ago as 20 January 1889 the **Bromyard News** was saying, "What would we not give for a Bromyard News of 1789 and will not our residents of 1987 look back with interest on our pages?"

A more direct way of looking back is given in this book. From a very large number of photographs lent or given to us we have made a selection to show what Bromyard was like between the 1880s and the 1920s. We have arranged it as a perambulation round the town which you can follow on the map on the back cover, finding at some points there are temporary diversions.

Basically this is a picture book. We have added narrative where we thought it essential, useful or even amusing, but we hope that for the greater part we have left the photographs to make their direct impact on you, uncluttered by our thoughts. As you look at the people in these pictures, starting with the gallant gentleman posing on Petty Bridge in plate 1, can you doubt that they were a vital community?

All introductions must end with a note of gratitude to those to whom thanks are especially due, firstly the publications sub-committee who prepared this book. A list of those who gave or lent us photographs is printed elsewhere. There are three individuals who must be named: Mr John Kinsman took great care in preparing our photographs for the printer; Mr Harold Thaker gave us unstinted help with the lay-out, and our greatest debt is to the Bromyardian who served on the sub-committee, Mrs Daphne Davies, to whose energy and persistence this book owes much.

Deborah Waller.
Chairman, Bromyard & District Local History Society.

Welcome to Bromyard in 1893 when you could stand in the middle of the road with your whippets, looking at the Petty Bridge toll gates. Turn round but do not expect to see the by-pass, that is many years away yet. Instead there is the row of cottages in which can be seen the pediment of the Gas Works. Bromyard, the hub of the universe for miles around at this time, had its streets lighted by gas from the 1870s.

Above left, a longer view. At the bottom of Linton Lane, opposite the end of the cottage row, is the house that was once the Bridge Inn, above right. Tradition has it that the Bridge, once a coaching inn, was where the Royalist officers were billeted when Charles I stayed at Tower Hill House. The men camped at Little Froome.

In Sherford Street, below, public and private life ran easily side by side. The house with the pediment on the left is the old gaol. Opposite top, the Congregational Church, built in 1701, was one of the first in the country.

Mr. Amiss's works, as can be seen from his billhead, came later.

The girls of the High School, bottom, did not move to Sherford House, opposite the old gaol, until 1899 from what is now Pettifers in High Street.

ESTABLISHED 1842
Sherford Street, Bromyard

MEMO. from **WILLIAM AMISS**
Monumental Sculptor

The school was started in 1893 by Miss E.M. Martin, seen on the right with members of her staff. It closed in 1906, despite its highly trained teachers, perhaps because its fees, 1½ - 3 gns a term, had been criticised as high in 1903.

Below, private life - Mr. Edward Lashford Cave, solicitor, about to go out driving from his home, Park House, with his wife and a friend. Mr. Edmund Williams, whom we shall meet again, is at the wheel. Opposite above, Mr. & Mrs. Cave and family in their conservatory.

Below, imagine in August 1910 when a traction engine, drawing two loads of bricks, almost toppled over and then went out of control. People driving uphill turned and galloped towards the bridge closely followed by the engine. In time it was pulled up at the Gas Works.

Round the corner into the Square which, as the focus of social and commercial life since medieval times, has seen many gatherings of townspeople. On Whit Tuesday, 5 June 1900, Pretoria Day was celebrated with a pageant. Led by the band and the horse-drawn fire engine the procession made a circuit of the town finishing at the Grammar School where the children and the aged poor were given a substantial tea by Mr. Barnes of the Cafe.

The workaday Square. Below, just before the day begins on a summer morning; note on the extreme right, Mr. Perkins' shop which was demolished in the Thirties.

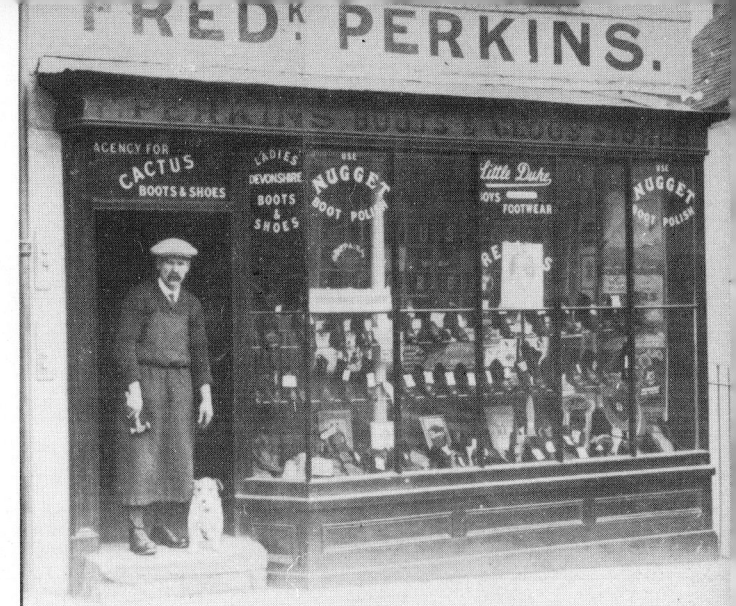

Above, Mr. Perkins himself; as well as boots and shoes of all kinds he made surgical footwear.

The Square was the market square, as can be seen left from the stallholders, now packing up at the end of the day.

Into Broad Street past the old Post Office, above, run by the Bennett family for 61 years.

Left and opposite, two of the "numerous and good" shops, as a traveller described them in 1885. The ironmongery was one of the many enterprises of Mr. Pettifer, whom we shall meet again.

Two views of this half of Broad Street from each end.

Mr. Pettifer's clothing shop is the one with the blind, above. The Wine Vaults are on the left, below, and the Progress Stores, a drapery, on the right.

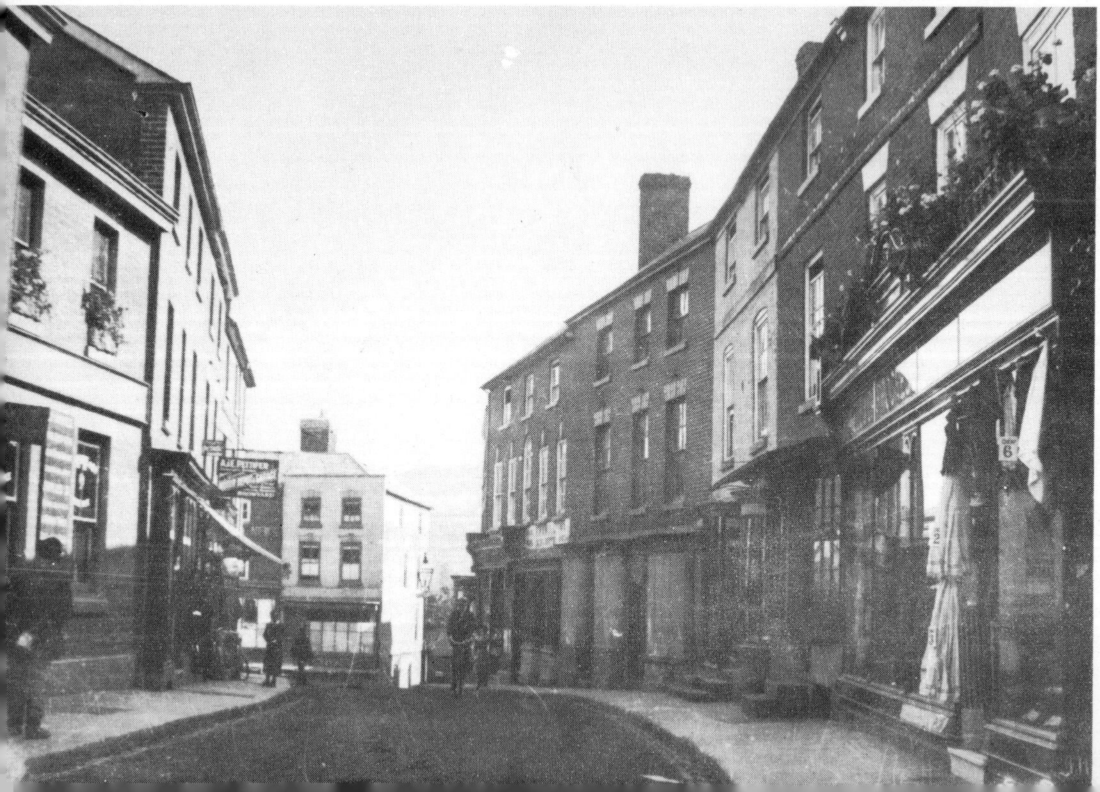

BROAD STREET. BROMYARD.

On the other side of the bend ....

FALC

.... to Market Day.

The traveller also said, "The inhabitants of all classes in the politeness of their manners afford a pleasing contrast to those of the manufacturing towns".

The Falcon, covered with plaster, was said by the **Bromyard News** in 1883 to be "moulting" and it was to be hoped that it would be allowed to shed its false coat to appear again in its original and picturesque black feathers.

Lloyd George, then Chancellor of the Exchequer, with his wife, one of their daughters and another lady, took tea at the hotel in the early summer of 1909 on the way to Wales. Their car was said to be " a handsome one ".

A few weeks later in August crowds turned out to see General Booth of the Salvation Army, in a white car, drive through the town on his way to meet the Bishop of Hereford.

Go round the Falcon corner and there is Nunwell House, left, but not known as such until the early 19th century. Previously it was an inn, the Seven Stars, and returned later to the comfort and succour of humanity when the front of the house was used as the doctors' surgery until 1961.

In Pump Street, below, was one of Bromyard's staple industries, the Tannery. Mr. James Jenks of the Tan House (the one with the shutters) was said to be "in a splendid way of business as a tanner" in the mid-19th century. The Tannery operated into this century - Mr. Perkins bought leather there - and its chimney towered over the town.

Just beyond the Primitive Methodist Chapel, right, is the turning into Victoria Avenue, only half of which now stands since the construction of the by-pass. Tower Hill House was once a girls' school. As can just be seen through the wintry branches it was covered in plaster which was removed by Dr. W. O. Wells, who lived there from 1920 to 1936, making the house look more as it may

Bromyard, Pump Street.

have done when Charles 1 was said to have stayed there. Linton Lane goes down from the top of Tower Hill and branching off it is Frog Lane, now cut in half by the by-pass. Here was the first St. Joseph's Roman Catholic Church, below left. Below right is the remarkable man who built it with his own hands, Father Denys Mathieu, O.S.B. Clock maker, electrician, inventor, he was one of the original seven monks who went to Buckfastleigh to build the present Abbey.

Also in Frog Lane he put up a presbytery, a parish hall, a bungalow and converted two railway carriages into homes. He erected a church and caretaker's house in Bishops Frome. For his retirement he built a bungalow on Bringsty. He died in 1935 aged 76.

Left, Tower Hill from the top, outside the high stone wall of Froome Bank. This house was bought by Cadburys in 1906 as a convalescent home for their women workers, some of whom can be seen in the bottom picture resting in the garden. On the outbreak of war in 1914 the property was accepted by the War Office as a military hospital. After the war it reverted to a convalescent home. In 1935 it was bought by the County Council for £2,000 and became a children's home.

Turn into Highwell Lane and go past the Manse. Right, in its days as a Primitive Methodist Chapel; someone ought to have got to work in the garden with one of Mr. Pettifer's scythes.

Beyond the Manse is Oldditch, used for all kinds of activities from revivalist meetings to circuses and Strickland's Fair. Opposite, it can be seen in something of its former magnitude before the by-pass was cut through it.

The New Road where, in 1913, residents complained of the Croft being used as a pleasure ground and for travelling shows. Two years later the News & Record described the road as "the fashionable quarter of Bromyard". This was at the opening of the Picturedrome, the town's first cinema, on the site of the present police station.

Right, a gathering of Wesleyan Methodists in front of their church which was built in 1857. The porch was added later.

A quick turn down Little Hereford Street to see them tyreing wheels at the black-smith's, J. G. Sirrell & Sons, in 1912. Clouds of steam hide the wheel as water is poured over the contracting metal tyre.

Back into the New Road and round Guess's corner, left, to look along High Street.

One of Mr. Powis's plate glass windows, right, was smashed on a Tuesday morning in 1924 when a horse and trap backed into it, the harness having given way.

In 1893 Mr. Henry Pumphrey, seen below right, found that his shop did not meet the needs of his fast-increasing business so he took it down and erected the building below left. It had new dress-making rooms where about 20 girls were employed, some of whom are seen above.

Another old-established family business, also dealing in seed, corn and coal. James Whitsey Williams came from Worcester and founded the grocer's shop in 1844.

HIGH STREET BROMYARD.

Left, looking up the street to what is is now the car park. Rather formally dressed, the orderly boy, right foreground, cleared up the horse droppings. It was said he did not work fast enough, at a U.D.C. meeting in 1905, when his wages were 6s. a week.

Right, the water cart has broken down, some time in 1912, so mind the dust!

Below, the chimney of the Tannery can be seen above and beyond the Bay Horse. Then covered in plaster, the Bay Horse, with its spacious stabling for travelling stallions, was the recognised stud house for the district.

Mr. Edmund Williams, whom we have met, was an early motorist and garage owner. The front of his premises next to the King's Arms, see following page, shows the change in his trade from one form of transport to another within a few years. Mr. Williams served on the U.D.C., for a time as chairman and also as chairman of the water committee. Many of his photographs appear in this book.

Below is Angel Place, demolished in 1957. Angel House, on the right, was the childhood home of the late Mr. J. G. Sanders whose father was a tailor. Mr. Sanders described the house as "heavily timbered similar to the Falcon and Tower House .... There were three rooms downstairs, one of which was my father's shop and the only one visible from Cruxwell Street or 'Top of the Town' as it was very often called. The house had three bedrooms and an attic .... Mrs. Maddy's house was also of oak timber, but much larger than ours because it had two bedrooms over the archway which led to the blacksmith's house, shop and pentice, and garden plots for each house at the back, but the blacksmith's premises were not part of Angel House ...."

Round the left hand corner into Sheep Street (now the Old Road) where the sheep markets were held. On May Day, the 29th of the month in Bromyard, h ere there were maypoles decorated with oak boughs and flowers, and the dancers wore oak leaves.

Right, Bromyard Queen Nancy, steam traction engine made by John Fowler of Leeds, seen here with a load of shoddy for the hopyards. The engine was new in 1909 and a common sight round Bromyard until 1934 when it was retired to The Tiffins, Pencombe, home of the late Mr. Jack Smith, machinist and haulage contractor.

The Piccadilly Toll House at Flaggoners Green, left, demolished in 1966.

"Come and have your photographs taken!" cried someone in 1911 and the girls of York Road came.

Milvern Lane, left, does not look deserving of the "unenviable reputation" it was said to share with Sheep Street in 1899.

The Toll House, right was built in the mid-18th century. Note the bird cage below the lamp; the bird warned the toll-gate keeper of approaching travellers.

At one time Bromyard was said to be noted for fat beasts and laying main sewers! Certainly both appeared in the thoroughfares at one time for the former were sold in Milvern Lane and High Street until about 1889 when the sale of all livestock was moved from the streets, where it had taken place for centuries, to yards behind the White Horse. This was because of the success of the annual twelve stock sales, organised by the Bromyard Market Company, which now became fortnightly ones. After improving his yards next to the White Horse Mr. Sampson could accommodate 400 beasts and over 1,000 sheep. His bullock sale in November 1890 was said to have "the largest and best collection of cattle yet offered at one sale in this part of the country". In 1893 the old-established firm of Worcester auctioneers, Bentley, Hobbs & Mytton, held their opening sale of stock in the "New Market of Bromyard", which was the northern part of the present yard adjoining Kirkham Meadow. The coming of the railway also helped the market to become a focus of the life of Bromyard and district.

Bromyard Record,
April 12, 1900.

"On Thursday last Mr. Knight
was favoured with a capital
entry of stock numbering 138
head of fat and store cattle,
377 sheep and lambs, 94 pigs
20 calves."

"On the same day Bentley,
Hobbs & Mytton had an
entry of 94 head of fat and
store cattle, 326 fat and store
sheep and lambs, 47 fat and
rearing calves, 167 bacon pork
and store pigs."

Prices fetched were fat sheep
up to 57s., wethers 48s. 6d.,
ewes and lambs 54s., fat
cattle, "very neat prices",
ranged from £21 5s., to £14 15s.,
cows and calves up to £16;
bullocks £12 10s. by the bunch.

These photographs were
taken in the 1920's.

Cider-making at Upper Wacton

Shearing at Wacton

Shepherding at Keep Hill

Poultry at the Wells.
1901 - Eggs, 16 for 1s.

Back to Cruxwell Street where the vet's house, the small shop and the Green Dragon are no more, but the Victoria Cafe still stands as the Dairy. The Victoria Cafe and Hotel was built by Mr. Richard Phipps of Buckenhill in 1889 as a temperance hotel to provide good fare at very low prices. Later the Social Club and Reading Room for working men was opened on the premises. Soups were served and smoking was allowed for 1d admission. The second concert, held on 17th December, was said to have been "crowded to excess".

The Church Institute, inside which a celebratory whist drive is shown below, is also a reminder of Mr. Phipps' generosity for he built it in 1895 during the construction of the Bromyard-Leominster railway. Appalled by what he thought was the filth and drunkeness of the navvies, he provided them with this building for wholesome recreation and rest. When the line was completed he gave the hall to the Parish Church.

Mr. Phipps, whose family were brewers in Northampton, and his wife came to Buckenhill in 1881 and from then on the life of Bromyard was punctuated by their public-spiritedness. Where there was want - of a snow plough to clear the streets, of food and fuel in hard times, of money to restore the Parish Church - the Phipps satisfied it. And Mr. Phipps provided Bromyard with its first piped water supply................

.... from this idyllic setting, right, in this view anyway, but in its time the Three Mills was a power house. Here Bromyard's corn was ground for centuries. In the 1880s and 1890s, thanks to Mr. Phipps, as a pumping station it augmented the town's erratic water supply, and then from 1900 to 1960 provided all of it from springs at Buckenhill. During the mid-19th century the pool was used for baptism, by total immersion, by the Baptist Church.

Above, a happy occasion in the water engineer's family.

Children interested in the delivery horse, as usual, right, in School Lane. Note the gravestones over the wall in the churchyard.

Nº 3   BROMYARD CHURCH   E. Williams Bromyard

On the two previous pages we have arrived at St. Peter's Parish Church, first to find the Reverend William Martin, vicar from 1877 to 1913, outside the Norman doorway; he is remembered especially for his work in effecting a restoration of the building. The carving of St. Peter, above the arch, is older than the doorway. The interior of the church shows the old pews in place, they were removed in 1912. The South transept was converted into a Chapel of Remembrance in 1919 as a memorial to the men who were killed in the first World War. In 1933 the East Window was replaced by the present one given in memory of Mr. T. V. Philpott.

Right, the Cottage Hospital, now Schallenge House, established in 1869 and finally closed in 1919. It averaged 37 patients a year and the accommodation of 5 beds was said to be sufficient for the district. The building may be medieval in origin and, as it was formerly called the Toll House or the Tollshop, probably the place where market tolls were collected.

Below, Mrs. Lushington, wife of Prebendary P. A. Lushington, vicar from 1927 to 1934, with a victorious group at the Vicarage front door.

Here we meet Mr. A. E. Pettifer again, the first man in
Bromyard to both own and drive a motor car; right,
in his 8 h.p. Belgian Lynx. He was fined 5s. in London
for driving without a man with a red flag walking in
front of him. His enterprises prospered despite a
disasterous fire, see below, to his Rowberry Street
premises in 1905; as well as his two shops they
included his garage with its fleet of cars and buses,
running the first motor mail vans round Bromyard
and a bus service. Another first of his was the
introduction of electricity to Bromyard in 1922;
two 20 b.h.p. crude oil engines drove the dynamos.
Fifty houses and some street lighting were being
supplied by 1924. Unfortunately the engine house,
between Broad Street and Rowberry Street, also was
destroyed by fire.

Mr. Pettifer and his staff outside the new Rowberry Street garage.

Below - "Nuff Sed", the popular char-a-banc.

An early bus, above, and one of the mail vans, below.

The power house before and after the fire.

This fire engine, right, was kept in Rowberry Street and used until the end of the 19th century. It had to be manhandled to fires and its pump was worked manually. Shortage of water was always a problem. Eventually a horse-drawn engine was bought, and sometimes that caused another problem - catching the horses.

We are now in Church Street, outside the Addyman's private door.

The Post Office, right, built by the local builder, Mr. Bill James, and opened in 1911. Also a view of Sherford roof-tops.

Two views of Church Street. Above, before the Police Station was built. Below, with the Police Station and the carrier's carts, the old Railway Inn was formerly called the Carrier's Arms.

At the end of Church Street was Bromyard Grammar School. It began as a chantry school in 1394 and after the dissolution of the chantries, was granted a charter for its refoundation by Queen Elizabeth 1 in 1566. It became co-educational in 1914. To allay the fears of those who opposed the idea of a mixed school the girls were provided with a separate entrance, and the sexes were strictly segregated in the playgrounds. In 1969 the Grammar School was merged with the new school at Ashfields.

Below, boys with a master, 1879/80

The Bromyard Divisional Police Force, above. In 1887 it consisted of a superintendent, two sergeants and seven constables, and this appears to have been the strength for some years.

Below, children waiting to go into one of the Bromyard School Treats at the Public Hall. This building, which had dressing-rooms and a caretaker's house, was built in 1859 as an instititute for working men and also for entertainments. For many years it was the place for much of the social and communal life. The Volunteers used it for drill and band practice before they had their own premises in 1906. Meetings, lectures, dances, concerts and profess-ional entertainments were held in it. There were murmurings for a new hall in the 1900's, but this one survived until 1922 when it became a cinema, eventually called the Electric Theatre under the management of two colourful people, Tom Diacoff and his wife, Madame Diacoff. The building was burnt down in April 1931.

The Volunteers, of which Mr. E. L. Cave, whom we have met before, right, was commanding officer in the 1880's. "D" Coy., 4th Herefordshire Rifle Corps, was formed at Bromyard in 1860. Below is one of the excellent bands they had during their history, about 1890. Overleaf is another from the 1900's. Leaving their annual camp in 1903 so rough was the crossing from the Isle of Man that some Bromyardians made their wills and gave up hope of seeing their loved ones again. The return from camp always caused great excitement. The Bromyard News described in August 1899 how crowds were at the Station to meet the train and children rushed to carry guns and parcels "so that the bandsmen have the latitude to 'give forth' with a spirited march". From the picture overleaf some of the atmosphere can be sensed.

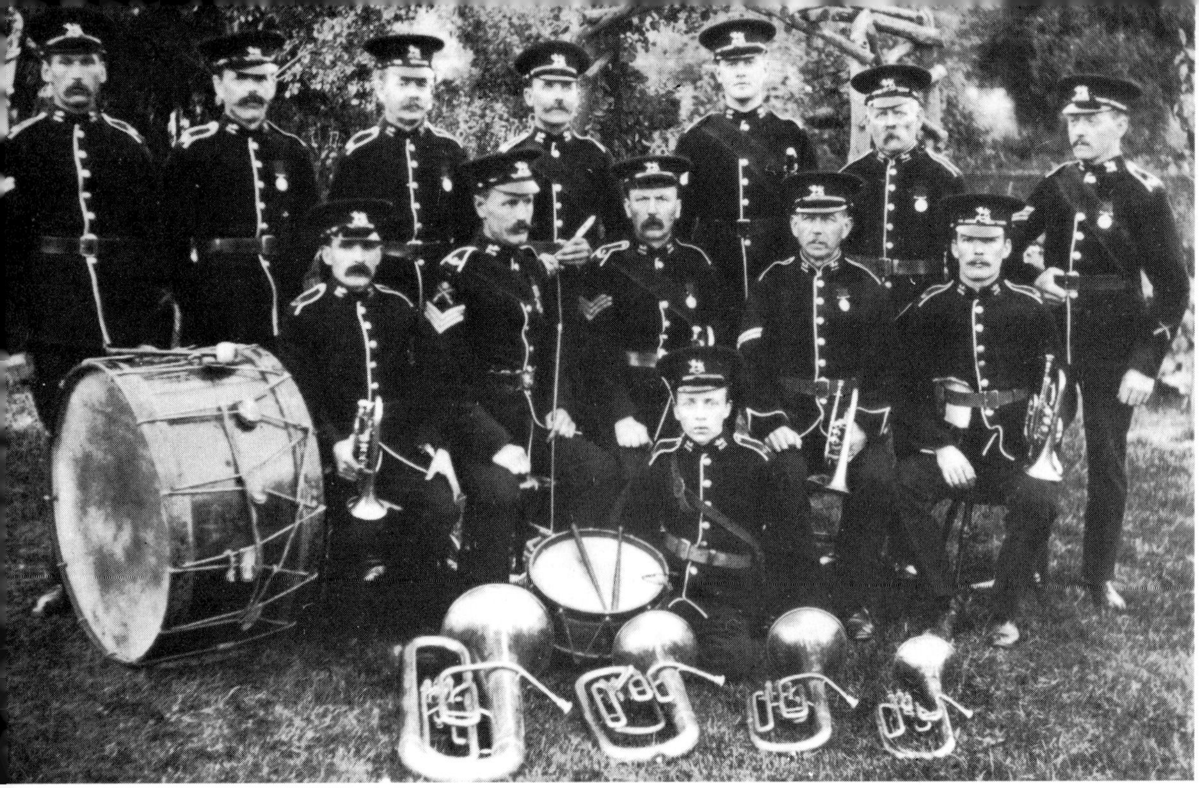

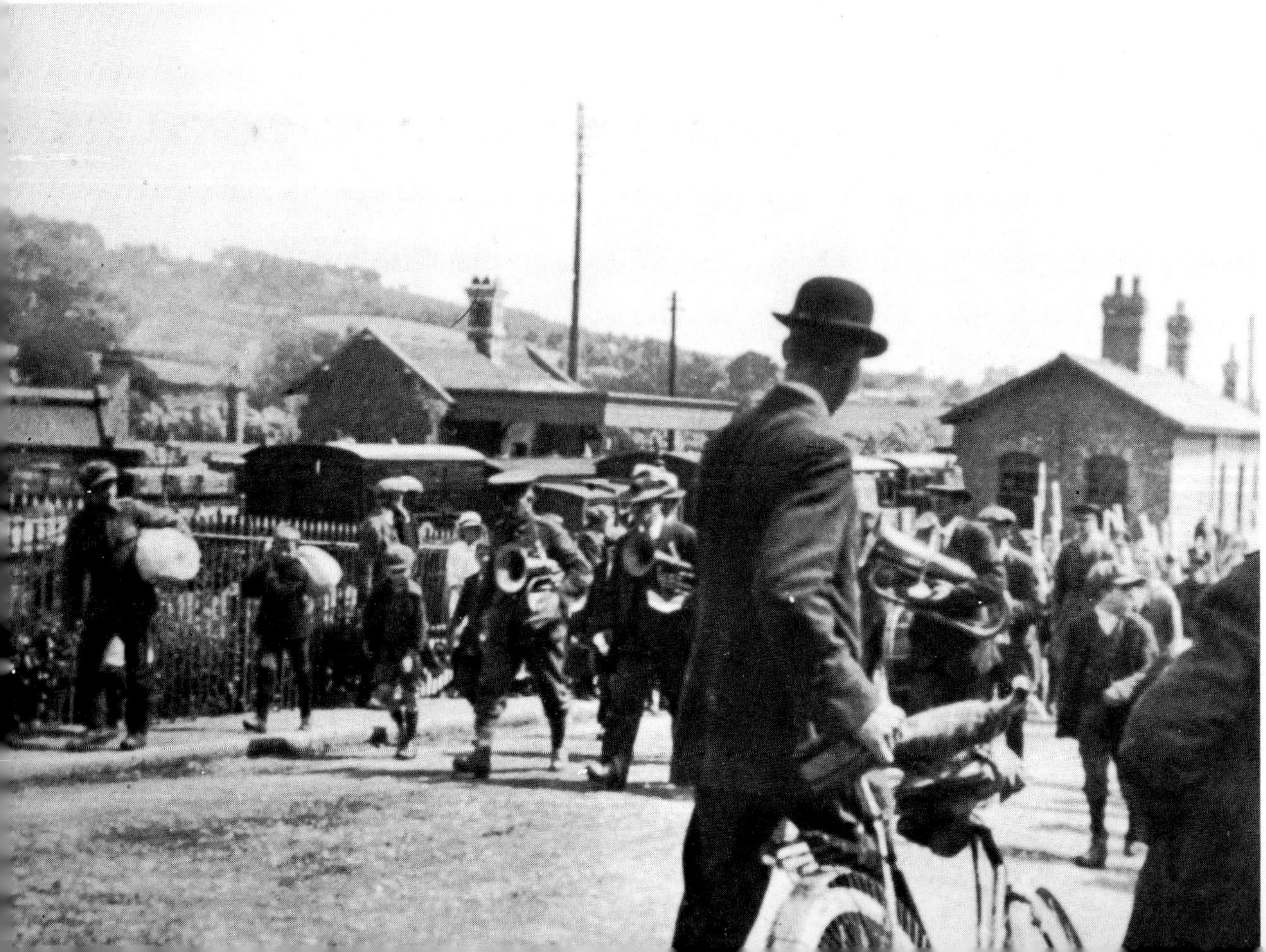

"On Wednesday, August 5, 1914 as the church clock struck eleven 47 Territorials under the command of Sergeant Bishop, in full drill order, headed by their band who played a joyous march, came down the bank with full military swing. All roads to the station were blocked with people. On the platform farewells were taken of relatives, the Territorials were in the best of spirits. Just before the train arrived the boys from the Council School were brought down and took their position on the platform. The men entrained quickly, the guard's whistle sounded and the train glided out of the station to deafening cheers, and to the strains of the National Anthem and three cheers." - Bromyard News & Record.

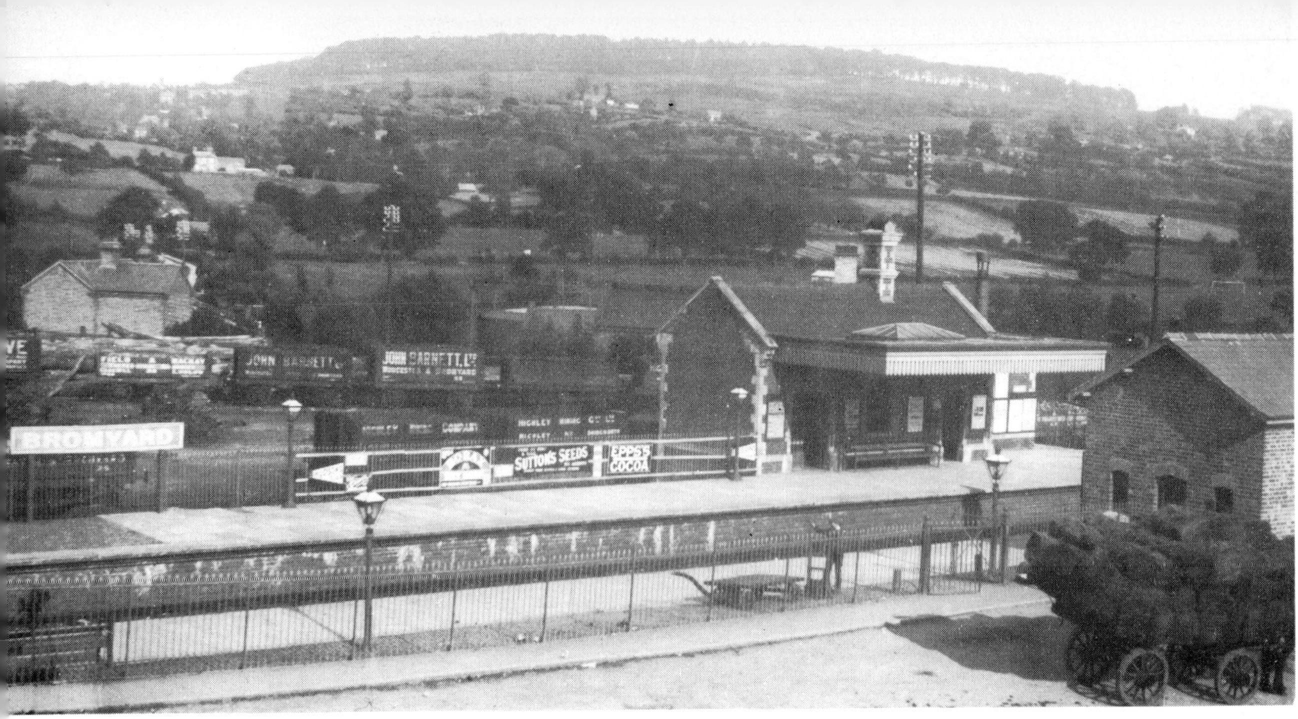

(500 Rms.—D) 1.—4-08.)
W. & S. Ltd.

GREAT WESTERN RAILWAY.

In reply to your | ______ Department, BROMYARD Station, | In your reply, please quote.

190

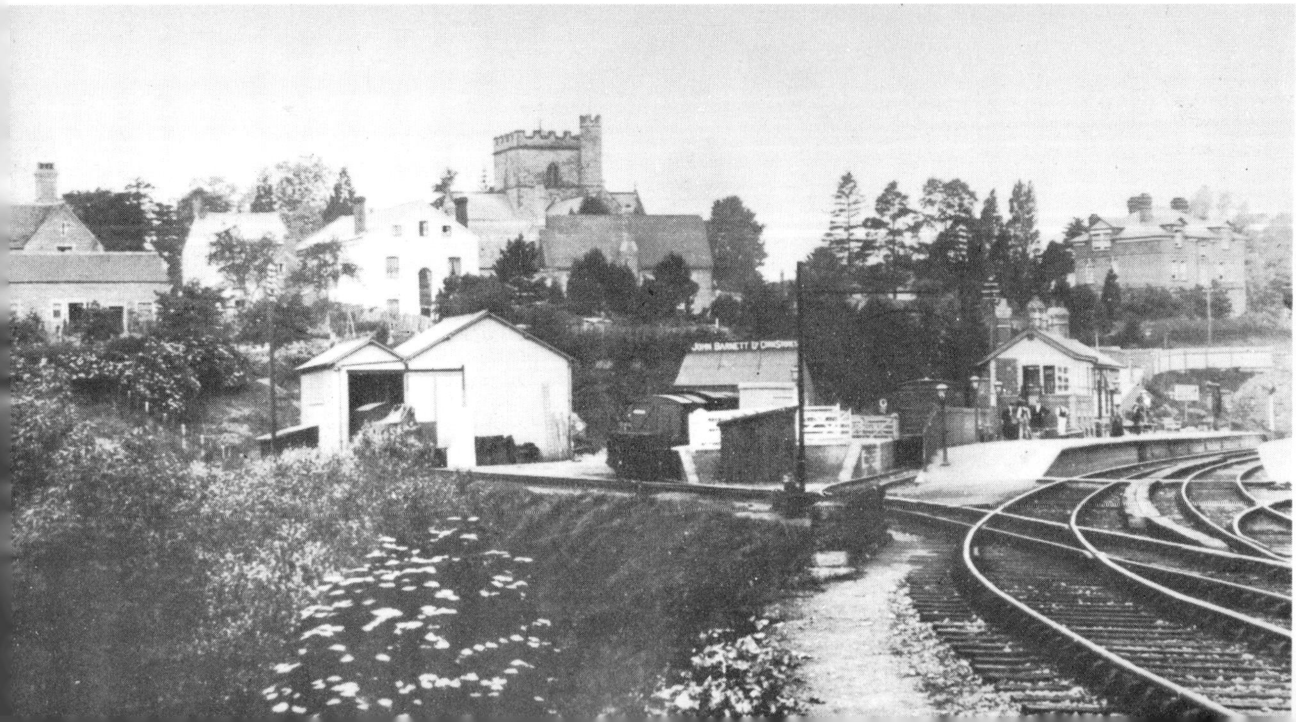

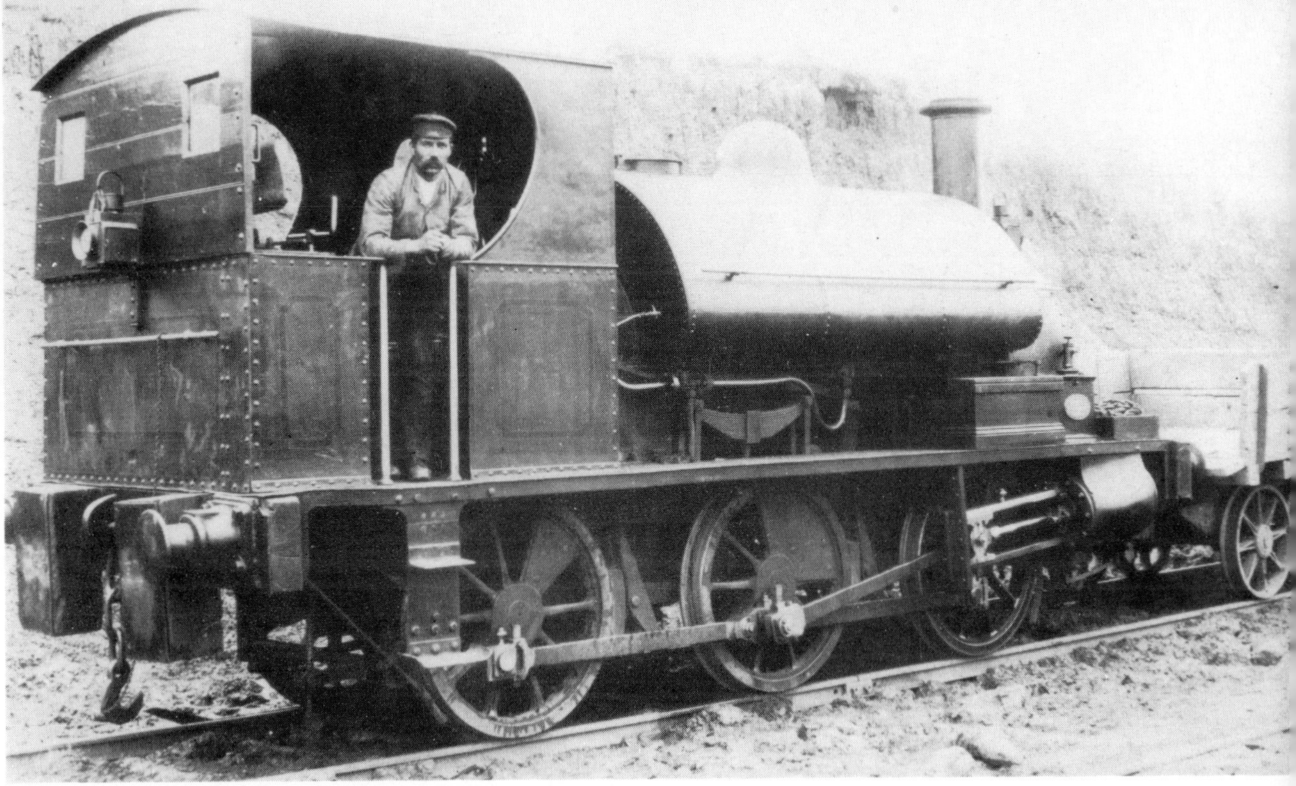

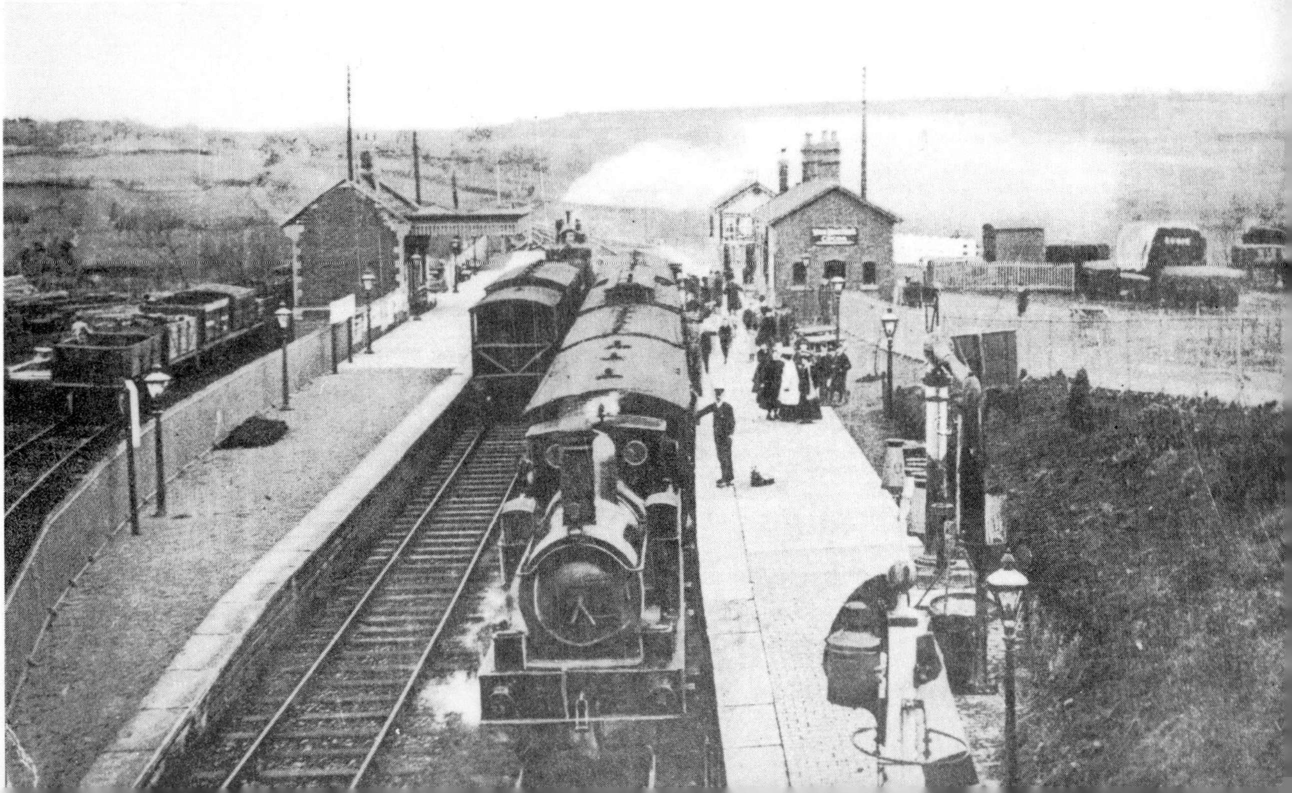

The above and the following remarkable photographs were taken during the continuation of the railway line from Bromyard to Leominster, the last one showing, among other things, the building up of the road from Broadbridge. When the line was finally opened in 1897 the first train from Leominster was met at the station by a large crowd headed by the vicar, the Reverend Mr. Martin.

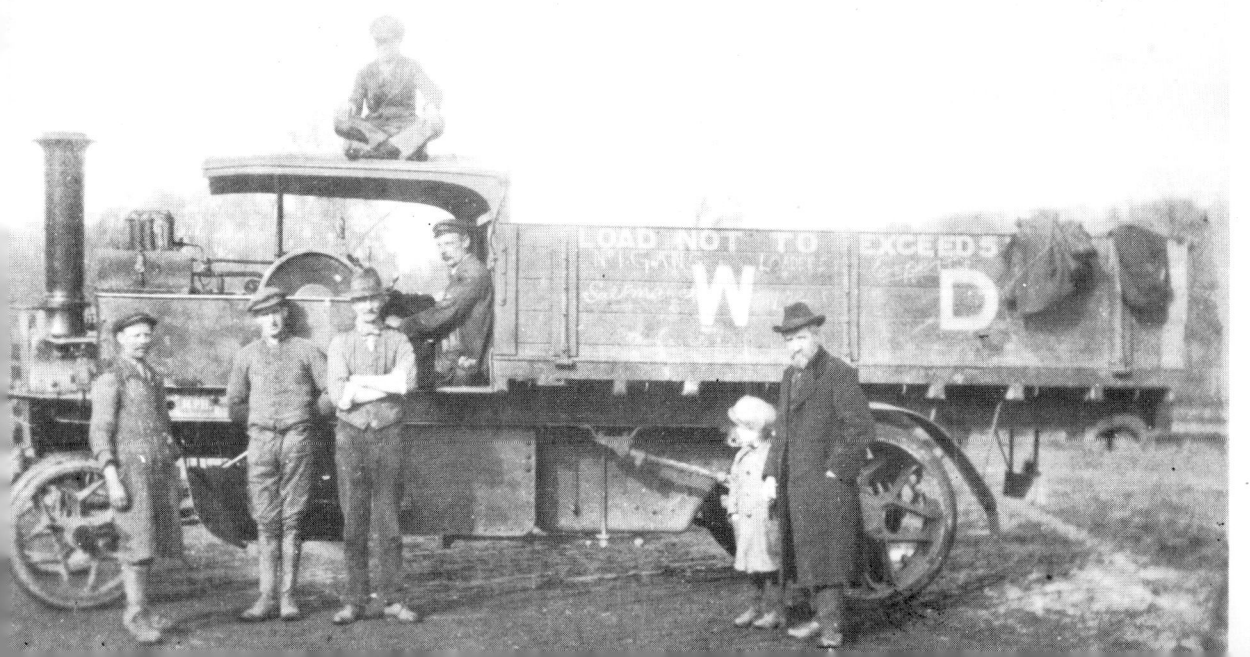

The railway, which ran to Worcester past the Stream Hall brick and tile works, helped the concern to prosper. Flooring tiles were supplied to the Admiralty and paving ones to the War Office. In 1914 the firm had the largest contract for paving tiles ever placed in this country by a foreign government for use on the Egyptian State Railways. Some of the local employees are shown above.

Below, the Saltmarshe Express, ex-Government traction lorry, which among other things was used to carry timber from Littlebridge to the station.

J. W. Williams' other department, showing their premises at the station, above. These buildings were erected between 1877 and 1914. The brick building on the left is the station goods office. The vehicles are Morris Commercials and carried animal feeding stuffs, grain, wool and coal. Below, hoppickers setting off from the station to the farms. Overleaf - "Clear 'em up!" the traditional cry of the pole-pullers to indicate it was bushelling time and the hops in the cribs had to be cleared of as many leaves as possible - the pickers can be seen in action, and on the opposite page local people out for an afternoon at the crib, a special kind of picnic.

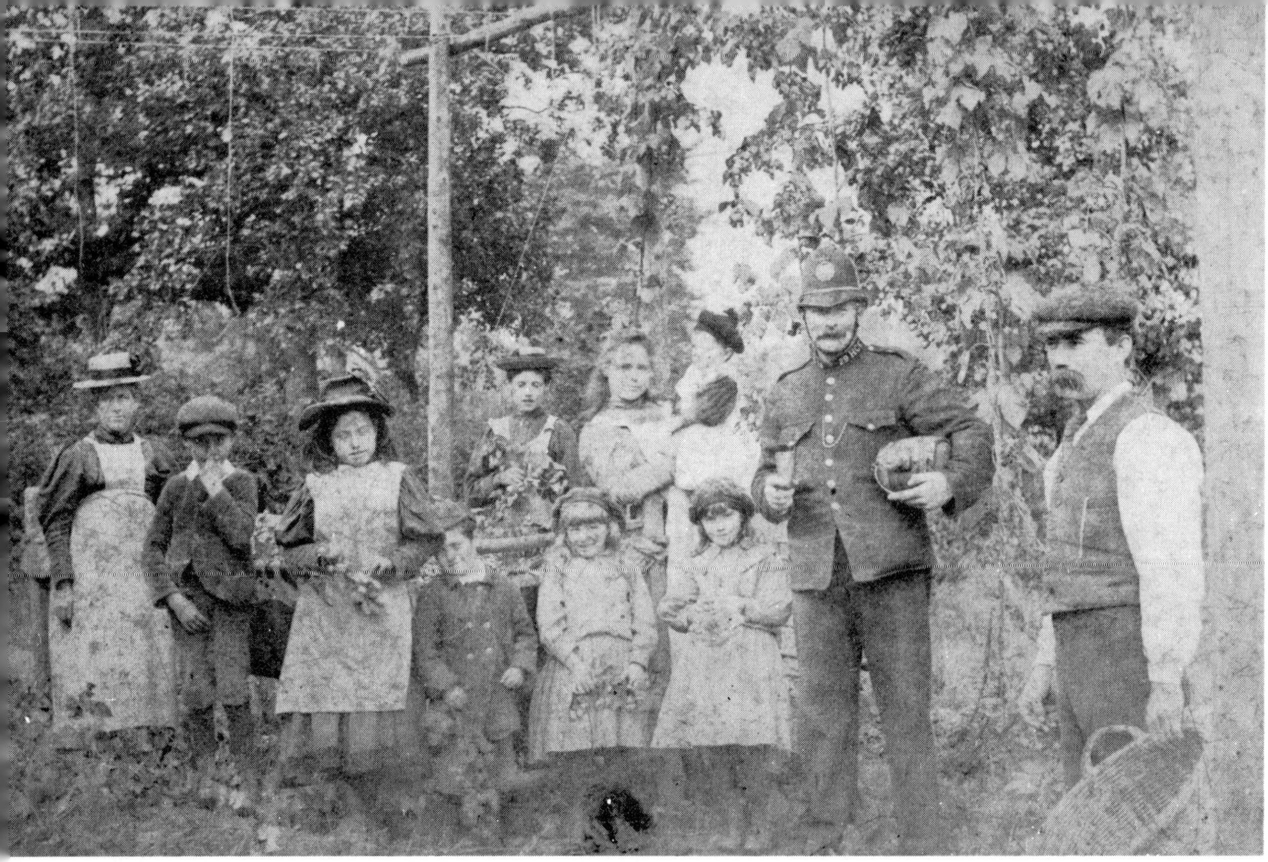

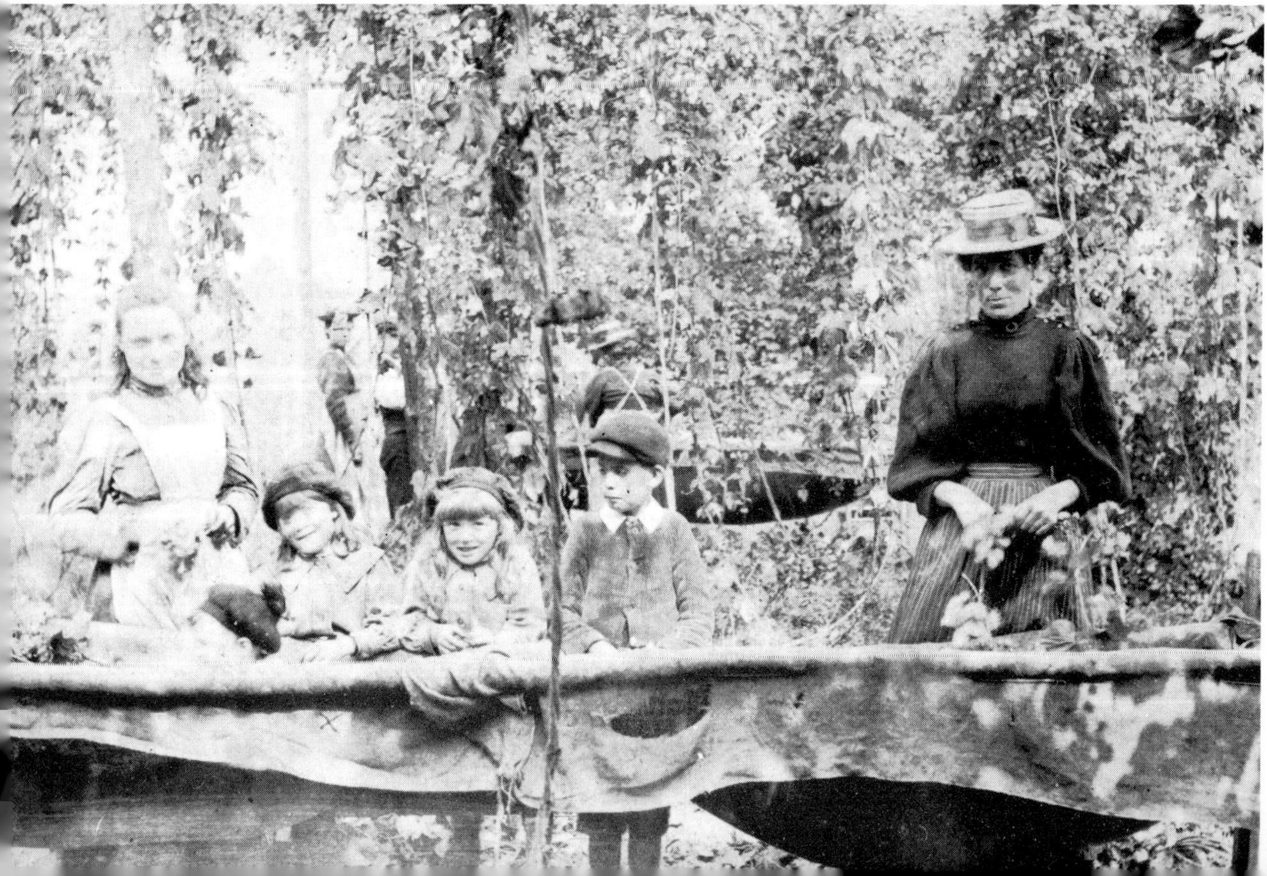

Two views of the road to Broadbridge, with its toll house which was built in the mid-18th century, before the coming of the railway.

Above, Broadbridge, dry: below, Broadbridge, submerged. The latter happened periodically, in 1924 to the extent of drowning sheep when in twenty-four hours 2½ inches of rain fell, representing 230 tons per acre.

Overleaf, good-bye, Bromyard, on a lovely summer morning, just right for a drive up the Rhea Pitch.

MISCELLANY

Some photographs in our collection did not fit into our perambulation, erratic as that may have seemed at times, but we felt they were too attractive to leave out. So there follows a short miscellany.

Tea in the bracken.

Below, Rear-Admiral and Mrs. J.A. Baker of Rowden House, and our old friend, Mr. Edmund Williams, are not really in danger of colliding.

Moving wheels of one sort and another.

Above, road works in the Avenbury Lane about 1912. They need to do something about the cyclist's road, too.

The pony and milk cart, below, are by the Schallenge gates in Rowberry Street.

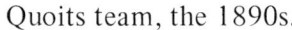

Bromyard Town, 1895.

Quoits team, the 1890s.

Bromyard C.C. 1905.

Bromyard Golf Club, with its
nine-hole course on the Downs
either side of the Kidderminster
road, was in existence from the
late 19th century to the last war.

BROMYARD
BOYS EVER
OWN
BROMYARD!

"THE BROMYARD DEWDROPS."